T0128033

TURADH

A BREAK IN THE CLOUDS BETWEEN SHOWERS

AILLSE CREAG (AILSA CRAIG)

BALBOA
PRESS

A DIVISION OF HAY HOUSE

Balboa Press books may be ordered through booksellers or by contacting:

Balboa Press
A Division of Hay House
1663 Liberty Drive
Bloomington, IN 47403
www.balboapress.com.au
1 (877) 407-4847

ISBN: 978-1-5043-1371-1 (sc)
ISBN: 978-1-5043-1372-8 (e)

Balboa Press rev. date: 07/09/2018

My book …

I wanted to write words
not filled with tears or a sad sigh
I wanted to write words
that didn't make you cry
I wanted to write words
that maybe brought you a smile
I wanted to write words
that are just happy, once in awhile
I want to take you places
you maybe not yet have been
I want to take you places
in which you can be seen
I want to take you places
that take you into nature's smile
I want to take you places
you may even see a crocodile
I'd love you to open my book
and just dream in a cosy nook
I'd love you to open my book
and get lost in a story and smile
I'd love you to open my book
let my words surround you
for a wee while …
- ailsa craig

THE CHAIR BY THE SEA ....

She sat there day after day
watching the dolphins play.

The chair was there for a reason,
it stayed in place, season after season.
Sometimes the waves would wash its frame
or the winds would try to push it in a game.
Its stance is crooked as its legs rot away,
no one has moved it, to this day.
It was placed there by an old friend,
whose broken heart was, trying to mend.
She would watch time retreat with the tide,
her sadness, was too hard to hide.
Now the chair sits all alone,
as time and tides took her home.

OUR ADVENTURE ...

Is there room on the path you travel,
imagine the adventures we could have.
Imagine diving into the deep blue ocean,
camping by a fire, with a glass of sav.
Imagine riding horseback in Mongolia,
or patting a llama in Peru;
touching the stars high up in Nepal,
so special to be sharing it with you.
We can just sit on a beach and hear the waves roll
and leave our footprints in the sand.
Or we can see the northern lights and play in the snow,
share our warmth in a distant land.
So please make room when you see me arrive
because there's no other path that is mine.
Together we can travel and experience so much,
together at last, it's our time.

YOUR STAR ...

Across the seas
you seem so far.
Across the sky
I can see your star.
It shines so brightly
on the ocean below,
as I sit in silence
and watch it flow.
I let my thoughts
ride on each new wave,
the star lights the way
to see you, I crave.
I float away
on the sounds of the sea,
as I close my eyes
I feel you close to me.

MY BOAT ...

With the wind in my sails,
I turn toward the horizon.
I know not where I'm headed,
but will know when I reach there ...
and that's where I'll toss the anchor.

SUPER MOON ...

When I look at the moon tonight,
in my thoughts I hold you tight.
Now a memory because of time,
I hope you are happy and doing fine.
I wish the moon would light a way,
back through time and to the day
when you walked into my night
and captured me within your sight ...

WHEN YOU WALKED BY ....

Stars lit up the sky
the moment you walked by.
I couldn't take my eyes
off you.
You slowly turned
and looked my way.
You won't believe
how it made my day
or can you?
I wonder who you are
apart from a shining star.
Where were you going
when I saw you?
Did you notice
the sparkle in my eye
that day when you walked by
and I noticed you.

IF I ...

If I sail away
on a summer day
or dive into deep oceans
of blue.
Will I find you?

If I sit under the shade
of a beautiful tree
or lie in the soft sand
down by the sea.
Will you find me?

If I write a wish
and hold it in my hand
or write a message
in the sand.
Will it reach you in another land?

If I sail away
on a summer day
and the breeze guides me
across the sea.
Will you wait for me?

FAMILIAR ...

When I dive into
your words
it feels so
familiar...

TIME'S VEIL ...

The veil of time
thickens
after another cycle
passes.
Can I reach through
and touch
our lost moment
one
last
time

COMPASS OF OUR DREAMS ...

Sailing off on a whim
of a dream,
over oceans so blue
they mirror the hue
of skies up above.

We follow the stars
that light up the night
and point our sail boat right
in the direction of
our dreams ...

YOUR WAVE ...

You are poetry
in motion
and I can feel
your words
wash over me
and carry me
within you ...

TO MY MUM ...

A few years ago,
you drifted away
I still wipe the tears
to this day.
You were with me
from when my time begun
and now you are no longer
my dearest Mum.

Where the sunset greets
the rising moon,
is where I hear your familiar tune,
and I know you are near.

UNCERTAINTY ...

Listen
to the
whispers
that
encourage
you
into the realm
of uncertainty.
Uncertainty
is a place
where if you look
inside
you see where
you may like or not like
to be
but
the voices of reason
who think
they know
best
lure you away
from
within the walls of
uncertainty
and take you back
into
a world
that controls your true sense
of self
and labels you

Aillse Creag (Ailsa Craig)

with their sense
of you.
If you can
spend a moment
within uncertainty
maybe
you'll find
the key
to a life you are
wanting
to experience.

NOTES ON A PAGE TO YOU ....

Just let me sit ...
Let the world swirl around me
It has no need for my thoughts -
my 'me'
Open pages
Written words
No title
No ending
Just words
trying to find their way
to you –
to form a sentence
with an ending
Just let me sit
Let me bring you onto my page
Let our words dance together -
once again
Just like the music I hear
when I think of you
Forever playing in my mind
Forever reaching out to you –
with my words
Just let me sit
and get lost in an ending ...

CYCLING THROUGH LIFE ...

The images that surround me
as I cycle through the mist;
colours circling, colours dancing,
a feeling of love's gentle kiss.

I feel freedom in my vibe
and the wind through my hair
as the wheels of my life,
circle; circle without care.

I know my heart is full
of so many in my life.
I cycle with a smile in my pocket,
avoiding pot holes, leading to strife.

And as the mist disperses
and my ride comes to an end,
the voices of my memories
accompany me around ever bend.

I park my bike beside you,
as we face the trail ahead.
My tyres are worn and weathered,
easy to change though with band new tread.

The images that surround us
as we cycle through the mist;
colours circling, colours dancing,
the feeling you give me, from your gentle kiss.

YESTERDAY'S WISH ...

It's time to move on
from thoughts of yesterday;
thoughts that drowned me in emotion,
so wonderful to experience in a way.
It was nice to imagine
how I wish it could have been.
Reality is reality though
and my vision of you is tucked away
in a dream.
So, as I look around
with my two feet
planted firmly on the ground.
I'll find my joy in another thing;
things that give me pleasure,
things that make me sing.
Life gives some a dream,
a dream that makes them smile,
but for others we get a token view,
maybe, every once in a while.

VALENTINE'S DAY ...

I slid down
a moonbeam
and danced
through the stars
the moment
I saw you
and now
your sunny smile
lights up my world
every day

THE STORM ...

As the rain came down
and the thunder roared,
the lightning lit up the room.
With an almighty 'crack'
the palm tree snapped
as a ball of power
wielded its fume.
I saw shadows in the dark
come to life
as a light show
played quite near.
I felt the house shudder
as clouds clashed in anger
and forced submission to my fear.
As the rain came down
and our lights went out,
the party in the sky ensued.
The earth drank with delight
the beverage offered from above
and the clouds crashed and rumbled
as they moved.
When it was time to move on
nature packed up its band,
lightshow and drums in tow.
It headed over the hills and further 'in-land'
as we settled in sleep down below.

TRUST ...

Touched by the kindness
in his words,
she moved to open the door
to her heart ...

Moved by the serenity
in the calm seas of his eyes,
she swam through his soul
and reached his heart ...

Calmed by the gentleness
of his touch,
she found peace in the comfort
of his arms ...

Dancing to the music
she heard in his laugh,
filled her with the happiness
she so desired ...

The love she felt
when he shared his smile,
was mirrored on her face
as she closed the door
behind her ...

THE MOMENT ...

When the rest of the world
disappears
and all I see is
'you'

When I see the sunrise
in your eyes
and I know it's a new
'beginning'

When my heart beats quicker
at the sound of your name
and I look at you
'in wonder'

I realise 'you' are the reason
for my smile

TOMORROW'S LIGHT ...

Sea shells and sandy shores
Sea birds and ocean floors
Foot prints left behind
Tides of tomorrow uncover the find
Ships on the horizon, passing at night
Adventurers and travellers,
revelling in dawn's first light
Warm air of a summer's day
The freedom enjoyed
by dolphins at play
Sunset colours and holding hands
Lasting looks from distant lands
Stairs that lead up cliffs so high
Tears that flow when we kiss goodbye
Tomorrow's light will greet the day
and my heart beat will skip -
when you look my way.

DRIFTING ...

Guitars play
on a blue summer's day
Memories of you
in the tune that I hear
Softly the notes
strum on my heart strings
Playing a melody
I haven't heard for so long

Drifting away
as the waves lick the shoreline
Drifting away
as the guitar feeds my soul
Drifting away
on the breeze of a memory
Drifting away
on the music you play

INTO MY DREAM ...

When I close my eyes
all I see is you
and I take the path
into my dreams so true
You came into my life
and turned it upside down
Then you just walked away
I wear the mask of a clown
I long to see your face
and your eyes so deep
Just wander into my life
I'll be yours to keep
I want to feel your presence
when you look my way
My heart will beat once more
and our smiles will play
When I close my eyes
all I feel is you
You take my hand in yours
and our hearts go too ...

IF I WAS A FAIRY ...

I'd like to be a fairy
and float amongst the trees.
I'd like to fly with magic wings
and mix it with the bees.

I'd like to wave my magic wand
and grant you what you desire.
I'd love to dance with nature's grace
or fly up mountains and go higher and higher.

If I was a magic sparkle
and you were my special glow,
could we fly together through beautiful flowers
and to the lonely, happiness we bestow.

I'd like to be a fairy
and be ethereal and sweet,
maybe even Tinkerbell,
now that would be a treat.

FREEDOM OF LIGHT ...

In the light of the moon
into my shadow I wander
towards a place
I have never seen …
I have no vision
or reason to follow
the path of my shadow
to where it does roam …

The cloak of darkness
enshrouds my path
I have no sense of who
I am …
It just takes me along
into the world of shadows
where no one is exempt
to stand alone …

When the light of the sun
fills the sky with colour
and life is seen for each role
it plays …
It feeds my shadow
with essence of wonder
and frees my soul
to dance on its own …

EMOTION ...

Open the window
Catch the wind
Float on a summer breeze
down to the sea
Let it wrap itself
around you
and throw you
into the waves
Waves of emotion
carrying you into
uncertainty
of love's sweet victory ...

ONE NIGHT ...

A song
A tune
A note
A word
A guitar
A voice
A memory
A place
A feeling
A look
A chord
A page
turned

FESTIVAL TIME ...

Packing my gear,
it's that time of year
and the music will play,
it'll be different each day.
There'll be smiles, there'll be chats,
peaks and wide brim hats.
We'll dance and probably sing,
interesting food and nibbles we'll bring.
Catching up with some chums,
folding chairs for our bums.
There'll be sunshine, there'll be rain
better pack the mac, once again.

STAND UP ...

Come on stand up and move
Fall into the groove
Let it lead you on forward
Forward let's go
Eyes straight ahead
Don't look behind
Those days are over
You are one of a kind
Look at you glow
If only you could know
Just how bright you are
Follow your star
It shines in the sky
'Like a diamond so high'
Lighting your groove
So, come on and move
No need to prove
To anyone who you are
Those who see your
Star shine
They are your kind
And you will find
Will walk beside you, always.

BROWN EYES ...

Brown eyes in the night
Brown eyes my delight
Brown eyes like pools so clear
Brown eyes into my heart
so dear
Brown eyes you stare into mine
Brown eyes I think you're divine
Brown eyes my light through
the haze
Brown eyes I'll remember you
always ...

A LITTLE CRUSH …

Sometimes
you feel like flying to the moon
but realise soon
that in order to get rid of the scars
you may have to fly to Mars …

It may take a bit of time
so, don't rush, enjoy the crush
and sip a cool glass of vodka and lime …
Sublime …

LIFE ...

Climbing trees, gravel knees
Secret cubby houses, throwing autumn leaves
Skating on puddles and riding through mud
Memories of my childhood and the times we've
all loved
Growing through teens and we know what
that means
Moods galore and slamming the door
Boyfriends and parties, dresses and shoes
Homework and exams
after school interests to choose.
Learning and marks, left us with worry
Until the last school day came and we were
in a hurry
to grow up and leave, to find something to do
Either bring in a paycheque and get some travel
in too
Then we meet 'the one', then he says goodbye
Our hearts are forever breaking, as we continue
to cry.
We work, we travel, we love, we care
Sometimes 'the one' stays and we think we are
'there'
Our lives start to change, as we have to pay bills
We go on to marry, pay a fortune for these thrills
We find a home to start a family together
and one by one they appear, new loves to love forever
And then it restarts, as the wheel again begins
The children enjoy some play but may hurt their shins.

On goes life, we experience so much,
either alone or with friends, family and such.
We look back in wonder, at all we have done
As life slips away from us, but for others, it's just
begun.

MAGIC EYES ...

Your eyes, so lovely,
in the night
They weave a pathway
of sprinkled light
Their magic realms
are deep in hue
The colours of the depth
of light in you
Whoever gets to travel
through the tunnel
of your eyes
Will be transfixed
by their magic
and be mesmerised
by you.

THE SURFER ...

With grace, you stand
You bend, you move
The wave grabs you
in its power
as you ride its strength,
its spirit
in towards the shoreline
Its shadow lurks behind you
trying to instil fear
so you'll fall
and its watery hand will clasp
around you
then toss you into
the angry foam of its fury
as it crashes into the sea
But you master its strength,
you master its power;
you are mesmerized by the wave,
by the thrill of being a part of its
journey
and ride this beauty
until it can give no more
and you are the victor,
the master of the wave,
the master of your board
The board complies with
your moves,
your grace,
your skills.

Aillse Creag (Ailsa Craig)

> Together you are one
> and the waves bow with respect
> and the battle never tires
> and for the onlooker,
> it is exhilarating …

SOUTHERN OCEAN BREEZE ...

Turquoise colours of the sea
Rugged cliffs stand on guard
Waves crash on rocks below,
dancing high in the air
providing a beautiful vision
of free spirit
Glass like tunnels form
as the waves curl
to unfold
Seals are playing
jumping in and out of the water
and surfing in on the waves
Toes tingling in the icy waters
of the southern ocean
Shells adorn the shoreline
and seaweed provides colour
and the smells of the sea
The sky is so blue
and the winds pinch your cheeks
like a memory from childhood days
Nature's natural beauty
at its best ...

WAITING FOR YOU ...

Smoke haze room
shadows in the light
A hum of voices
music cruising around
in the background

Waiting, waiting for you now

It seems like an eternity –
maybe it is,
maybe it is as it should be

I still feel you close –
feeling like I do
about you
Your cologne fills the air –
it surrounds my memories

Waiting, waiting for you now

I look for you
in all the corners of my life
in every song I hear,
in every book I read,
in every touch I feel.

Waiting, waiting for you now

The music plays
I sway
as I look into eyes

I don't recognise
and shadows I don't see
in a place that was once
just ours

Waiting, waiting for you now

THE FIRE PLACE ...

Fire place's warmth
on a cold winter's night
Blankets and doonas
and snuggled up tight
Book about others
their lives and their love
As the fire starts crackling
and sparks fly high up above
A warm cup of cocoa
is like love's gentle hug
The cold felt in your fingers
is warmed by the mug
We curl up close
as the rain falls outside
and the cold hands of winter
can't touch us, even if they tried
The fire is warm and
it draws us in near
So lovely to be with you
It's so cosy right here ...

MY SHINING STAR

And here you are
you rose like a shining star
above the dark clouds
that surrounded me
and all that I could only see
was you …
and then you looked my way
upon that magic filled day
You wiped away the tears
that lived within my heart
and gave me a reason to start
to smile again

SOUNDS OF THE SHELL ...

I put a shell
upon my ear
I had been told
it was the sea I'd hear
Immediately
I was taken away
with the tune of the waves
on a bright summer's day
I closed my eyes
and danced in the sea
I had no care
who was watching me
I danced and I danced
with the shell to my ear
My escape to the ocean
within the shell,
its magic so near...

DON'T GO ...

Stay there
don't look away
Please don't become a part
of yesterday

The way you sit
upon your chair
The way you play fondly
with my hair

The way you grab me
with your laugh
It makes me giggle
like when you tickle my calf

The way you touch
it makes me shiver
The way you look at me
makes me quiver

Please stay awhile
and just be mine
Just bathe in this moment
we have together in 'time'

LA MER

La mer is beauty –
her colours, her moods
her turquoise dress billowing
in the winds
as she roams from
shore to shore
seeking her one true love
Her call can be heard
by those who know her
Her heart can be felt
by those she captures
within her trance
Once enticed into her world
she weaves her magic
and takes you to a special place;
her sanctuary
You dance within the hypnotic
movement of her gown
as she wraps her colours of blue
around your senses
and when her dance does stop
and the seas go grey
you know
she can no longer hear
her lover's call
and you find your heart
feels the chill and waves of tears
that now fill her world

Upon the day he returns
her call,
the beauty of
the hues of blue
will once again adorn
La mer

FREE YOUR DESIRE ...

The whisper
in your heart
Once you speak of it
you have to let it go ...
Once it's free
it will seek the heart, the place
that is home...

A MOMENT IN SILENCE ...

To sit in silence
is to go for a walk within
Close your eyes
Close your mind to the world
that surrounds you
and breathe
in and out slowly.

I feel the stillness of my world
It's pale and soft in colour
I find myself always by the sea
with a mist of calmness
around me.

My thoughts ride in
on the crest of a wave
and break gently on the shore,
touching me
with splashes of colour;
each separate with their own
sense of importance.
As I touch each one
I contemplate its make-up
and set it free.
Some go back to the ocean
and seek a new wave.
Some walk beside me
and give me strength.
Some I let go
they don't belong with me.

Aillse Creag (Ailsa Craig)

I am in a peaceful state
within
as I can see with more clarity
the pathway
to my horizon,
my place of true existence.

COME WITH ME ...

Come take my hand,
let's go to adventure land.
Let's follow the path
through forests of trees,
look for four leaf clovers on our knees.
Let's climb that mountain
and check out the view.
Let's just sit on a rock ledge,
just me and you.
There's a row boat by the jetty,
let's row across the lake.
It's so blue and peaceful,
many photos we can take.
Come take my hand,
let's just sit here on the grass.
A moment spent together,
a moment in time that will sadly pass.
Let's close our eyes and lie here,
and wait until night time falls.
We can jump from star to star,
until reality beckons and calls.
We can float amongst the moon dust
and dance along the milky way.
Come take my hand –
into another day.

SAILOR JIM ...

I'd heard the story
about old sailor Jim.
He has grey whiskers and hair
and many a tale he can spin.
His jumper is woolly
with time worn holes,
from hooks on fishing nets
or hanging off poles.
His eyes are as blue
as the ocean he does roam.
His heart is warm
within which many have found 'home'.
He is a legend to all
and a friend to most.
His boat is always in sail,
he welcomes you on board, such an
interesting host.
I met him one day
while walking the pier,
we shared a warm smile
and stories I loved to hear.
The sea is his love,
the wind is his friend.
Only stopping for awhile
if his sails need a mend.
We chatted and laughed
that day on the pier.
His life is a story book,
and there's not much he does fear.

Turadh

In need of no map,
he steers away from any land.
He sails via the stars
and leaves no footprints in the sand.

IF I LOOK AT YOU ...

If I look at you one more time
with my feelings waiting to be set free.
If I look at you one more time,
will you give your hand to me?
If I look at you one more time
and you smile at me the way you do.
If I look at you one more time,
will you know my smile is only for you?
If I look at you one more time
while you build castles in the sand.
If I look at you one more time,
will you come with me to wonderland?

If you say yes to me with your eyes
and your smile melts my well-worn guise.
Will you warm my saddened heart
and know it's not forever, if we should ever have to part.

NEPAL MAGIC ...

The streets were small and dusty
and incense filled the air.
There was music around each corner,
a mixture of chimes and guitars would pair.
There was so much colour and noise,
as cars beeped their way through the crowd.
There were shops full of clothes and trinkets,
the owners beckoning to us with a voice so loud.
The atmosphere was mysterious,
full of stories, people and spice.
I have never felt so excited to be here,
with friends who were ever so nice.
We were tempted by the momo and lassis,
Dal bhat and chai tea as well.
Kathmandu was a story in the making,
that I couldn't wait to share with family and tell.
Our adventure was only beginning,
the mountains of Nepal called our names.
We embarked on a life changing journey,
full of beauty, perseverance and some pains.
We'll never forget our moment
that was shared in the magic of Nepal.
It was hard to say farewell to our story,
our memories though, will forever in us dwell.

AUTUMN ...

Colours of Autumn
orange and brown
Leaves gently falling
on the ground
Crunching through piles
that lay on the path
Throwing them in the air
and having a laugh
Change is coming
and we prepare the way
Nature will rest and recover
until Spring has her way
But for now
we wait for Winter days
when life will slow down
through cold fogs and misty haze
Change will come
and colour will too
Just for now I'm content
with the colours of Autumn's hue

HER TEAR ...

He broke her heart
the day when he did part
and just walked away
into another day
another tomorrow
and she was left to borrow
a tissue to wipe her tear

BALIVO DAYS ...

We enjoyed our days
on our boat 'Balivo'
We'd be off so early
with our co-owner, Phil, in tow
We'd skim across the water,
it was like glass and so clear
Head towards the volcano
which resided quite near.
We'd steer past the islands,
the Bee Hives and the town.
Always nibbles and drinks on board
which were easily downed.
We'd laugh and share stories
and sometimes catch a fish
or half a tuna,
yummy sashimi on a dish.
The memories are many,
the days all too few,

Aillse Creag (Ailsa Craig)

the nights at Rapopo
with the usual social crew.
I'll never forget
the weekends out at sea.
The other boats/friends we would wave to
or Phil's famous fishing whiskey.
Esther would ring
and check all was ok
or if we'd had any luck
catching fish that day.
We'd arrive at Rapopo
and get Balivo back on land.
I remember jumping overboard
with the rope in my hand.
I knew it was deep
but was told to jump in.
I emerged from the depths,
clothes stuck to my skin.
Bev and Brian
at Rapopo would be,
waiting with drinks
after our day out at sea.
We'd sit there for ages
and enjoy the surrounds,
full of locals and travellers,
Toby, Sara, cats and beautiful grounds.
It's good to look back
and get lost in those days,
spent with many wonderful people
although some nights were a haze.
Most have moved on
our boat is no longer.
The memories made though
have only got stronger.

MY FEARS ...

When I was young
we would drive through a forest;
a forest of gums that
watched us go by.
They were a group of old souls
and stood tall, grey and just stared
and for a reason unbeknown to me,
I felt quite scared.
I felt they were calling me
and I knew if I went in,
that my life would disappear
and I'd never be seen again.

I loved the ocean
and swimming in the waves,
watching them curl and crash
was one of my faves.
But the ones that were mighty
in both volume and stature,
filled me with fear
that in their roll and curl,
it was me they would capture.

Once we skied on a mountain so high,
when a cloud took over
and we became part of the sky.
We had to stop and just be still,
we were in a white out;
a phenomenon that can kill.

Aillse Creag (Ailsa Craig)

You just can't tell whether you are up
or down,
completely white around you,
no sky above or below no ground.
We had to wait for the time to pass
before heading down the mountain
on our skies so fast.

One day I tripped and fell into
your eyes
but here I felt no fear
for within your eyes and beautiful soul,
it was a blessing to just disappear.

YOU ...

Your soul
is as graceful
as a wish on the breeze
and all who are touched by it
find a home forever in your heart.

Your wings
are like the lace of a beautiful
dream
woven together
with the threads of love.

Your voice
is like the gentleness
of a creek in flow
quietly guided to ears
open to your sound.

Your eyes
attract all who catch their gaze
Windows of beauty
always open to those
who can see
'you'.

MY TWINKLING STAR ...

It is through the stars
I travelled,
light years have kept us
apart.
My journey started
the day you were born,
it was the beginning
of our 'special' start.
I saw the twinkling light
in your eyes
from my faraway place,
so I've journeyed through
the universe
to immerse myself in your
beautiful space.
If our lives
are drawn together,
our paths will be guided
by our sun.
No matter how far
we are from each other,
our hearts have already
begun,
'to be one'.

TRACKS IN THE SAND ...

Pathways
and broken dreams
All is never
as it seems
Masks galore
available for hire
Easy to pick one
to match your attire
Seagull tracks
criss cross the sands
Planes fly high
to distant lands
Eyes that meet
on a summer night
See through the mask
you wear ever so tight
Where we travel to
is where we go
Leave your mask behind
and be who you know
The eyes that travel through your soul
or hitch a ride
on the wing of a seagull
will love you
for who you portray
when your mask is off
or thrown away.

IT'S ALL YOURS …

It's sad when some things
come to a close
that have been the reason
for your smile.
To find something
that gives you pleasure
only comes to you
once in a while.
Then the dynamics change
and you sense a move is
close by.
You realise it's you
who needs to move on,
even with a tear in your eye.
To leave behind a reason
as you ask yourself, "why"?
I guess it's like the change in season
and something else will surely
come by.
It just takes another
to take away that joy.
I wonder if they realise
and it's just part of their ploy
to make you think
you're just an unessential part of the crew.
Please know there will be something
better
that they can't take from you …

Aillse Creag (Ailsa Craig)

For Great Uncle Charlie who fought in Gallipoli …

I can't imagine
the fear you felt
when you scrambled
up the cliffs,
with bullets whistling
passed you,
hoping that they'd
miss.
Seeing some of your mates
lying wounded on the sand,
knowing each of those injured
would have given you a
helping hand.
You got wounded in the leg
but still you battled on
and ended up in France
with your mate,
another Australian son.
Your blue eyes ever so bright
but much sadness captured,
within their sight.
You were such a brave
wee soldier.
Our appreciation of you, steadfast,
even as we grow older …

MAN IN THE MOON ...

Man in the moon
you watch us play
as we skip from star to star
to get through each day ...

You look down and smile
and provide a light
as daytime journeys
take us into the night ...

SMILES ...

If I can jump over the moon
and run into sunrise
I might find you there
within the smiles
that greet me today ...

TAKEN ...

I am angry at yesterday
for snatching you
away
and hiding you in a dream
I've yet to find ...

ALWAYS ...

My heart has never
left your side
It found a place
which felt like
home ...

MOGHRAIDH (MY LOVE)

If I close my eyes
and go within
our memory
I see you fade
into the mist;
the mist of the highlands.
It carries you away
and with you,
you take my heart.

I search for you
in my dreams;
are you lost within
the many corridors
of my life?

Aillse Creag (Ailsa Craig)

Find the door
that unlocks the passage
back to me
and once again
it will be just you and me
against the world.

I sometimes find you
in our cove.
I can sense you.
When I hear the waves
break on shore,
I see you running towards
me
with that smile that lit
up my world.
I reach out to touch you,
to feel you again,
but you disappear into the misty spray
that moistens my eyes.
My tears forever tattooed
within my sight.

Do you wait for me,
wherever you roam
in the hills of our home?

The years marked in time
have been many.
You left no space in my heart
for another.
You are my life,
my journey's end.
'Moghraidh'

WHEN MUSIC PLAYS ...

When I hear music play
it adds flavour to my day.
I travel on the notes
to faraway dreams
and listen to the words
which hit me like magic beams
of love, sadness and goodbyes;
nothing like music to give you
smiles, tears, and sighs.
I dance a little
and let myself go.
The room becomes my stage
as I move to and fro.
I might do some ballet
and imagine I'm free,
swirling and turning, or bending
my knee.
Listening to the beat
sometimes I just dance,
I could be in a smokey club
perhaps somewhere in France.
So, where the music takes me
depends on the song,
it will take me away
to where it knows
I belong.
I love it.

MY MORNING WALK ...

I lock the door
and set foot on my
well-worn morning path.

The sun stretches out
its rays of golden light
as it yawns and peaks
over the mountains.
It kisses my skin
with its beautiful morning
warmth
and I feel good.

My music playing
in my ears,
gives me an extra spring
to my step.
I feel like dancing, running,
I feel free.

The morning chorus of car noise
accompanies me.
An ambulance speeds past
and I worry about the occupant
or to where it's going.
As I turn towards
the hills,
my mind is faraway.
The songs take me back
to happy memories.

I smile a lot, I cry a lot,
I think a lot and I try to morph myself
back
to wonderful places I loved.

The usual morning groups
of walkers,
from many nations,
exchange smiles, waves, nods and greetings.
It's lovely to see them
each day,
all so different.
I see each of them as a story book,
I would love to read.

Lots of dogs this morning,
all happily panting,
pulling their owners to each and every
plant, tree or blade of grass.

I wipe my tears,
happy tears
and on I go.
My home, my space,
my morning.

MOMENTS IN NATURE ...

When the sun shines
on your smile,
the whole world
lights up ...

When nature's perfume
hits our senses,
we are transported to
a place of serenity ...

When the rain clouds
wash the earth
and refresh its thirst,
a feeling of renewal
arises ...

When you take my hand
and look into my eyes,
my whole being gently sighs
and I am happily trapped
within your natural charm ...

TO TREK ...

To climb
To sigh
To step
To stop
To breathe
To step
One
Two
Three
Four
To persevere
Again
Once more
To stop
To breathe
To smile
To look

Aillse Creag (Ailsa Craig)

What a view!
What a view!
And on we go
So worth it
Phew

MY LIGHTHOUSE ...

As I steer my boat
away from broken dreams
I trust the light ahead
is all that it seems
It gives me passage
through a sea full of tricks
and many hidden obstacles
seen as harmless antics
I am guided by the light
The darkness has no moon
It starts on a faraway shore
I hope I will reach it soon
If I keep to my course
and sail with the wind
I'll reach my place of dreams
before my distant lighthouse
beam
is dimmed

A MEASURE OF TIME ...

I wanted to feel with
my arms
what I was feeling with
my heart
I wanted to sit beside you
before we had to part

I wanted to just talk
to you
and find out who you are
I wanted to just walk
with you
but we didn't get that far

So now I just write words
to you
words I wish you could
hear
but I know not where you
do roam
if only you were near

I wanted to just
love you
because I felt
your heart
I wanted time to go away
but the time came to part

REMEMBERING YOU …

Remember the days
when love would bloom,
our hearts would flutter
when you walked into the room.

Remember the days
we would laugh and be silly,
splash each other with water
and hug when it was so chilly.

Remember the days
we just loved to feel as one.
We would hold each other tightly
until the arrival of the morning sun.

Remember the days
we travelled overseas.
We wandered where the wind did take us,
through mountains, villages and forests of trees.

Remember the days
after years had passed by,
you became so ill
I had to hide the tears from my eye.

Remember the days
when we held hands for the last time.
You gave me a smile
before you were no longer mine.

Aillse Creag (Ailsa Craig)

Remember the day
when our eyes were locked in goodbye,
I remember these days
with a smile, a tear and a sigh.

IN THE MOONLIGHT ...

As I look at the moon
tonight
I dream we dance together
in the light
I feel you hold me so close
and tight
which fills my heart with
such delight.

I see the beam that shines
from the moon
and feel your love
it makes me swoon
It's such a night to play
a tune
that will take our dance from
night to noon.

REMEMBERING YOU, MUM ...

The gentleness of your touch
so soft
against our skin
The colour of your eyes
so blue
like an ocean full of love

You surrounded us each
with love and tenderness
and protected us
as we began our walk
into life

We watched your moods
through the many trials
a woman faces

There were times of great loneliness
being so far from 'home'
There were times of great brilliance
shown in your creative abilities
There were times of anger/sadness
when days were tough
There were times of great love
caring for Dad through his illness

There was a time to say 'goodbye'
when you slowly slipped away from our lives

HE

He had admired her
from the first day of his employment.
He had served her dishes
of culinary desire.
The way she laughed
and
brought everyone into
her conversation;
into the realm of her demeanour,
made him crave for permission
to enter.
He watched as she moved,
like a ballet in slow motion.
He sought a safe place
to which he could divert
his gaze
away from where his heart
desired to stay.
He knew he had no chance
to be a part of
the happiness that played out
before him.
He knew he could only watch
in wonderment
as his desires remained in a place
that required a key
he did not possess.

THE FLOWERS IN YOUR HAIR ...

You wear the flowers
of the sixties
Psychedelic colours
are in your eyes
The years have added
many layers
and your questions
have now become
sighs
Your hair is grey
and thinning
A few lines tell
stories
on your face
Your smile though
does still
light us up
when music fills
your space
You belonged to
a time
when your spirit felt
so free
You found the gift
of nature
and then gave birth
to me

SEASONS

You are
my Springtime
memory
and
just like the
new buds
of the
season
you painted
my world
with colour

If I ever lose
my memory
of you
I will lose
you
and
walk back
into Winter

SHARED VIEWS ...

Smiles and tears
inside fears
Coloured tents
all in a row
Games played
high fives all round
Hiking the trail
or hitting the ground
Hair that's a mess
normal I guess
When the wind blows
and the waves do pound
The flight of the seabird
utters no sound
We walk together
and share the news
The top of the mountain
behold, amazing views
The dolphin that jumps
and swims by the boat
The singer on stage
hitting the right note
Within your sight
so much to see
Within your ears
'Can you hear me?'
Open up and let
it all in
Your life in amazing
so let us begin
to enjoy life together

BYDAND

(STEADFAST)

I wander through the forests of my home,
keeping out of sight, as I have learnt from my ancestors.
There's such a chill in the air
and snow still carpets my land.
My family feed nearby;
we nibble on any greens, twigs or berries
we can find with the onset of Spring.
My antlers often get caught in the scrub
and at times it's hard to break free.
Humans have built fences that often catch us off guard
and trap our freedom.
Humans also stalk us and use guns against us,
smiling when they take our spirit away.
I am proud
I am the protector
I will look you in the eye

I will fight for my freedom
and pass my brawn onto those who follow
in my foot prints.
I am a stag
I am a Gordon
I wear the tartan in my heart
I am the pipes you hear
echoing through the Glen.
I am the mountains of the Highlands
I am your strength, your soul
Animo non Astutia
(By courage not craft)

TIME BY THE RIVER ...

Sometimes I'll sit on the river bank
and marvel at the water as it absorbs the sunlight
and sparkles like a bag full of diamonds
I'll stare in wonder and dream
as I watch the dragonflies
dive and skim the surface
I'll jump on their back
and fly across the river to the other side
then let go and get lost in the leaves of autumn
gathered together to provide a safe landing
The atmosphere is soft with the hues of autumn
colours imbued in the surrounds
Here I dream so many dreams
Some are filled with people I've loved and lost
I cry silent tears
longing for
one more shared conversation
one more shared laugh

one more shared look
as we sit here by the river
But mostly, I am at peace
I enjoy the now which will one day
be now no longer
I catch the dragonfly flight once more
and fly high over the diamonds below
until I find my place
my place by the river
and just watch time drift slowly by

DO I USE MY WINGS ....

On the edge of the cliff
so how do I fly?
Do I spread my wings
and go high?
What do I do?
What do I say
to make the sun come out
and stay?
When I turn to look
at what's left behind,
are the shadows of my memories
enough to bind?
Or is it in the clouds
that I'll find
my wings to fly
into the sky
to be with you.

A EUROPEAN MEMORY ...

Red rimmed windows
line the street
with blooming flower boxes
looking ever so neat
Cobbled road ways
and solid wooden doors
Stone stairways and
black and white tiled floors
We wander down idyllic streets
as small cars and bikes whiz by
Somewhere for a drink would be nice
as people gather in a bar nearby
There's lots of laughter
and stories told
Wine and beer shared by
both young and old
What a beautiful town
we have found
I just love the pretty setting
and such a happy sound

THE ECHO IN THE ROOM ...

You go through the pain of childbirth
because you know there's a reward ahead.
The pain is to let you know you have received
a beautiful gift
but it's not going to be easy.

And then there's an echo in the room

You go through first days of this and that,
school, practices, games, performances.
You hold your heart in your hand
watching them and how they fare.

And then there's an echo in the room

You cook what they like,
you wash, clean, drive and listen –
not because you have to,
but because you want to make their lives
happy and to feel loved.

And then there's an echo in the room

You go through all their tests, exams.
projects, all their interviews with them
because you want them to succeed in life
and be proud of themselves.

And then there's an echo in the room

You go through laughter, tears, anger,
slammed doors, misunderstandings,
relationships and let downs
because you love and understand
what it feels like.

And then there's an echo in the room

You go through every doctor's appointment,
dentist, hospital stays, every injury, illness
because the idea of them suffering pain and
difficulties, is too hard to bare and you want
to take their place, take the pain away.

And then there's an echo in the room

You miss the walks, the talks, the hugs,
the kisses, the handholds, the meals together,
the drives, the shopping days, the birthdays,
the treats, having someone to be silly with.

Because there's an echo in the room

But then you watch them leave,
enjoy loving relationships, travel,
experience the joys of success, friendships
and families of their own.

And you know, the echo in the room
is all part of it and as hard as it is
to hear,
the echo, is worth all that it represents.

LET'S DANCE ...

When you dance with
the sun
you radiate happiness
and warmth

When you dance with
the moon
you will be in the spotlight
of your dreams

When you dance with
the stars
you will forever shine for those
who appreciate
your presence

When you dance
with me
I will never let you go

TO MY DAUGHTER

I gaze at her with such admiration
as she gently cradles her children.
I see the love that fills her eyes
and her heart
as she looks at each of them.
I feel the care she surrounds them with,
the loving hands of protection.
I see the love of her children
as they look into their mother's eyes,
it's a beautiful sight.
I'm so glad they have her
in their lives
to guide them,
to hold their little hands on their journey.
As her mother, I cannot be more proud
to watch how easily she lovingly
carries out her role
as their mother …

A mother's love

THE SIGN ...

I saw a message
on the beach
To me it seemed
so out of reach
A message painted in the sand
I hoped it was written
by your hand
As I got nearer
and saw what it did say
It was a sign from you
that brought a smile
into my day

LET IT RAIN ...

If the rains
do fall
on the summer moon

The waves
will rise
with each breath
I swoon

The leaves
may fall
from the tree of life

But the light
of the sun
will lead
away
from strife

MY CURSE

The door was ajar
I could see so far

What a view
and 'you'

Shyness grabbed me
and slammed
the door

My eyes went down
and
looked to the floor

The view ahead
and 'you'

No more

FINDING YOU, FINDING HOME ...

Tracking the winds
of your words
To find my way home

Climbing high mountains
and seeking the light
in your eyes
To find my way home

Connecting to your
heart
and clasping the strings
to your soul
To find my way home

Following the currents
and hearing your music
in the roll of the waves
To find my way home

Feeling your words
like a warm hug
by the fire
I will find you again
My home

OUR TIME ...

As the rains do fall
and the flowers bloom
and the light of the moon
shows the way
I hear your words
like a soft summer breeze
as it gently plays
with my day
I see your smile
in the colours of dawn
and your eyes
in the stars up above
I feel warm comfort
in the kisses you share
and the gentle caress
of your love

Will you stay by my side
for just one more day
until the mists of time
break this moment
we share
and again
take you away

SUN DIAL ...

Pirates and sail boats
guided by the stars.
Sun dials and time travel,
life before our scars.
Lights on the horizon,
maps to steer us home.
Messages appear
in many ways,
audible by phone.
Pirate's treasure
sparkles,
X marks the spot.
The line of the sun
determines,
how much time together,
we have got.

YOUR EARTH, MY SEA

Seeking your eyes of brown
caught within my sight
Seeking the darkness
for my light
You are the land
for my sea
Follow your path
to where I'll be

My seas of blue
seek the earth
in you
and
though we dwell
each day apart
my waves are the life
of your heart …

BE FREE WITH ME ....

Take a chance
come on have a dance
with me

Let's roam the
world
with words
unfurled
and be free

LA JOIE DE VIVRE

(THE JOY OF LIFE)

The many joys that laughter brings
Spending time chatting
to a heart that sings
Feel good moments
that last a life time
Friendships and memories
like a long cool glass of gin
with a spritz of lime
Long walks as the hours
slip away
Walking the dog
on a blue summer day
The joys of company
of music, of cheer
The feeling of friendship
when we all share a beer
'La joie de vivre' is ours
to live
Smiles and love
are ours to give

TIME TO SING ...

Time to sing you
a lullaby
with my touch

Time to sing you
a verse
from my heart

Time to sing
the words
of your smile

Time to just sing
because
you are a part
of my song

BUT, HEY, IT'S NICE TO DREAM ...

We always fall for the ones
we can't have
Maybe we can't face the reality
of it all
Maybe it's nicer to dream
about what could be
Not the actuality of
how hard the fall
We have the power
to imagine
A world with that dream
in tow
But when the hard facts
hit us in the face
Then we have to learn
how to manage the blow

But, hey, it's nice to dream

BREATHING SANITY ...

Questioning my sanity
Staring into infinity
Holding onto what's unreal
Maybe a dream
Maybe a nightmare
Breathing into the memory
Precious times
Precious words
Questioning today's dreams
Staring into clouds and streams
of thoughts
Following a journey of denial
Breathing out
Leaving sanity to find its way
towards a world that floats
on a wish from a dandelion
and that's where you'll be waiting
for me

TOUCH ...

The gentle warm breeze
of a summer kiss
The cool touch of
blue waves of bliss
The sweet taste of
fruits in season
The mountains we've climbed
for no other reason
than to be together
With just the touch
of your hand
It's not hard
to understand
Why everything comes
to life ...

DARK CONFUSION ...

The coolness of the night air
was wrapped tightly around me
Warmth was draining
from my body
An echo of the past
drifted into my ears
and got lost in the tunnels
of sound
I was confused in the darkness
My eyes were blurred
as I tried to focus
on a way out
I needed warmth
I needed to make sense
of the noise
I needed colour
I needed a sign post
that pointed down a path
into tomorrow

CLOSED ...

He was bewildered
when she closed the door
on his 'hello'
He didn't realise
it was he who had taken
the wrong turn
and read the wrong signs
that lead him
to this place
of 'no more'

TO DREAM ...

As we float amongst
the stars at night
Our dreams evolve
and within us take flight
We wander through places
meet people and dance
We smile, we fear, we feel
within our trance
Or we run from the shadows
that haunt our mind
Running and hiding
trying to leave them behind
Dreams are around us
in all that we do
In the places we visit
or even meeting 'you'
We float, we run, we smile,
we see
Within our dreams
the desires of our reality

TURADH

(A BREAK IN THE CLOUDS BETWEEN SHOWERS)

When the clouds part
and the sun shines through
I find my thoughts
are always filled with you

When the clouds part
I look to the skies
and see your reflection
in my eyes

When the clouds part
there's happiness in the air
The flowers start to bloom
there's colour everywhere

When the clouds part
you see smiles at play
and a feel of joy
at the close of day

When the clouds part
I see the words in my heart
carried on the breeze
far across the seas
to you

- aillse creag

Printed in the United States
By Bookmasters